AF470212

DESIGNING WORDS

Writing essentials for architects, artists & designers.

REBECCA W. E. EDMUNDS, AIA

Introduction by
Michael Alan LeFevre, FAIA

Published by Communicate Design LLC

First Edition

Limited of Liability/Disclaimer of Warranty
While the author, editors and publishers have used their best efforts in preparing this work, they make no representations or warranties with respect to the accuracy or completeness of the contents of this work and specifically disclaim all warranties, including without limitation any implied warranties of merchantability or fitness for a particular purpose. No warranty may be created or extended by sales representatives, written sales materials or promotional statements for this work. That an organization, website, or product is referred to in this work as a citation and/or potential source of further information does not mean that the publisher and authors endorse the information or services the organization, website, or product may provide or recommendations it may make. The advice and strategies contained herein may not be suitable for your situation. You should consult with a specialist where appropriate. Further, readers should be aware that websites listed in this work many have changed or disappeared between when this work was written and when it is read. Neither the publisher nor author shall be liable for any loss of profit or any other commercial damages, including but not limited to special, incidental, consequential, or other damages.

ISBN: 979820136375-8

CONTENTS

FOREWORD

"For heaven's sake, architects are artists. They communicate through their work. Why in the world would architects or artists need to write well?"

— Anonymous

If that's what you're wondering, then I'm glad we're having this conversation, because you need to read this book and master its lessons. But only if you are interested in saving your career.

I should know, I'm one of you, a design-, drawing- and image-driven architect who has practiced architecture since before Woodstock. I first started working in an architect's office at 14. It was May 1968. Seeing the modernist logo outside the small office above Heidi's Flower Shop in Plymouth, Michigan, I entered boldly. With only some fine junior high school drafting to communicate my skills, I began an internship with two lifelong mentors and friends and a life in the profession of architecture.

In the years that followed, I felt privileged to work with many of the world's finest architects in what has been a career now in its seventh decade. I have been a design leader and team member for two Progressive Architecture Design Award Citations (1972 and 1992), received multiple national and local AIA design and honor awards, been published countless times, and in 2012, was elevated to the American Institute of Architects College of Fellows for "advancing the profession."

In those years of practice, I lovingly worked my way through every medium of every era, beginning with hand drafting with graphite lead on vellum, evolving to plastic lead on mylar, Rapidograph pens and ink, pin at drafting, computer-aided drafting, and recently enjoyed a prominent role as a change-agent / disrupter / evangelist speaking nationally and internationally on the power of building information modeling and designer-builder collaboration.

Truth be told, I didn't see any of these professional evolutions coming, they just happened. But I was lucky enough to be there, eyes open, and willing to look, listen and embrace the power of each new medium as it transformed our profession. Perhaps I was, as Mark Twain called it: "a keener observer of life." But the one I never really saw coming was the power of the written word. It's one medium that has changed little. And It's the one that changed my life the most.

Over the past several decades, thanks to the advent of data reuse and the personal computer, I slowly became a better writer. Coupled with seeing the recurring failures of poor design communicators, I became determined to develop writing as a new skill. All this is prologue to my current role as managing editor at DesignIntelligence, a leading global think tank. Learning to write did more than just catalyze the many disruptive new practices I fostered over the third chapter of my career—it opened the door to a new career path.

You see, I'm here to tell you, my most recent shape-shifting experience has been to become a writer. And you should too. (Or find someone on your team who is.) Here's why.

While the most attractive aspect of architecture may be its foundation in visual and physical form—the creation of functional and beautiful buildings—we create them for people. And while the average Jane or Joe might appreciate a magnificent building, most of them lack the ability to describe it. Even fewer have even the foggiest idea of what we, as architectural alchemists, do in the sanctity of our mystery-cloaked design studios. We would do well to understand why. One reason is that we're taught to keep plying our trade a secret. We nurture and perpetuate our secret lingo—a world into which the unwashed public is not welcome. WE go to school for many years.... WE are the only profession educated in the arts, sciences and humanities.... WE are the public's protectors and arbiters of taste. With all this self-focus, it's little wonder many of us soon forget: it's the same public we've learned to exclude that we serve. Those same people—the ones who run businesses and industry—hire us to do their buildings. And we wonder why they don't understand us.

The reason our clients don't get us is because we speak different languages. They speak using those shared by the rest of the world: business, finance, numbers, politics and strategy. And wait for it, they can communicate. By deploying the fundamental communication skills most architects were directed to set aside when we started architecture school (speaking, writing) we began a long slow slide into illiteracy.

Well, enough of that.

The time for change is now. No matter where you are in your career, you still have time to improve your ability to think, speak, and yes, write well.

Where to start? To make the conscious decision to become a better writer, pick up a copy of this book: *Designing Words* by Rebecca W. E. Edmunds, AIA. Why Rebecca? Why this book? Simply because she is one of us. Architecturally educated, and a registered architect herself, Rebecca has crafted a unique, decades-long portfolio of experience teaching the country's finest firms and practitioners of all levels to craft and communicate their messages. In other words, how to write.

But there are plenty of legendary texts on writing available from Strunk and White, William Zinsser, Hemingway, et al., you say. Agreed. I have loaned or given Steven King's *On Writing: A Memoir of the Craft* to dozens of colleagues. Fine resources all. Get them and read them. But know this: despite these storied references' persistence in time, not a one is written by an architect for architects and other creative types who focus more on the creative process and result than on how to communicate about it.

What Rebecca Edmunds has done in her second publication, a sequel of sorts to her breakthrough book,

Architect+Action=Result: A Guide to Fellowship, Narrative and Meaning in Practice, is produce an approachable, hands-on resource for would-be writers from visual language disciplines.

In a compelling parallel to the *I Hate to Cook Cookbook,* Rebecca has given our profession a lifeline. In plain English, she has produced an easy to understand and even easier to put into practice toolset for architects and anyone else who wishes to become a better communicator.

Would you like to be better understood? Win more work? Explain and justify your design or creative rationale? How about differentiate yourself and become more persuasive in your presentations for the increasingly complex practice of architecture? One in which inclusion, diversity, and environmental and social issues are now expected?

Those without the ability to speak to their clients' interests and in their language will not survive. And here's the beautiful part: writing well adds no complexity; it reduces it. No software, hardware or apps are required. We all can read and write. No translation necessary! At least not if we do it well.

When it came time for me to write my book, *Managing Design: Conversations, Project Controls and Best Practices for Commercial Design and Construction Projects,* I was lucky to stumble across Rebecca, a colleague of Jeffrey Paine, FAIA, someone I was interviewing in my book. On a lark, I asked her if she'd be interested in chatting about a possible role as editor. Intrigued by the project (despite having to work with me), she agreed. Five years later, *Managing Design* has become Amazon's #1 bestselling new release in its category, and she has published her first book. Returning the favor after our first successful collaboration, she invited me to play a role as Contributing Editor. Now, with this release of her second book, a wonderful companion for aspiring architect writers, I am honored to offer this introduction. I can think of no one with a deeper list of satisfied clients or a greater capacity to write about writing for architects.

Do this for yourself: Learn to think, speak and write. Buy this book. It will help you do what you love—practice architecture. Who knows? It might even become another thing you love and are reasonably proficient at. Thanks in large part to Rebecca, it did for me.

I think it will for you too.

Michael Alan LeFevre, FAIA emeritus, Managing Editor, DesignIntelligence

INTRODUCTION

"I hate writing. I love having written."

– Dorothy Parker

Last year, I wrote a book about the process I've used to aid architects seeking national awards as members of the American Institute of Architects, Architect + Action = Result. After reading it, two artists from different states, who do not know each other but who are also clients, suggested that I extract the writing advice and compose a separate "little book" on writing. The artist who applied the term "little book" is a fellow Cornell graduate—a Cornell PhD—who chose the phrase in homage to the William Strunk Jr.'s self-published 1919 textbook for his writing classes. Strunk's volume, *The Elements of Style*, became a cherished writing standard—a lofty comparison to aspire to. While I'm certain I've achieved no such significance, my mission remains to aid the writing abilities of those of us who choose to study and work in disciplines that don't place writing at their core.

Before becoming an architect, I had no clue my career would hinge on anything other than my ability to envision and produce objects, be they fabric, garments or buildings—I was a textile and apparel designer first, then a writer, then an architect—all followed by a Master of Fine Arts degree in creative writing. Despite my educational sequence, the core of my practice as a designer, writer and strategist has always been to help individuals craft their professional narratives, no matter their purpose or pursuit, for their practices, careers, projects, awards, articles, white papers and books. I've also helped artists, documentary filmmakers, authors, educators and theatre directors. During these engagements, many clients discovered that their understanding of their contributions or approach to their work transformed during the process. In many cases, those recognitions and revelations meant more than their original reasons for seeking me out to help tell their story. As a result, I wondered, why not make writing and storytelling basics accessible to all designers looking to articulate the meaning and purpose in their work?

Honing your grasp of punctuation rules and sentence structure to frame cohesive, comprehensive writing on design or artistic work will serve you well regardless of your pursuit.

DESIGNING WORDS

Artists, designers and, especially, architects might not get the connection between a Master of Fine Arts in creative writing and the studio cultures of architecture and design. To help them in making that connection, I inevitably chip away to expose the myopic "specialness" of any single academic and professional endeavor. Why? Because the more diversity of thought you are exposed to, the more you realize the commonality between many human and artistic pursuits. Put simply, many Master of Fine Arts curricula have the same studio culture (called "pods" in the program I attended) as design and fine arts disciplines.

Writing has countless parallels with making and creating. In my own pursuits, I like to envision things, determine how to construct them, and then build them, preferably outdoors in work clothes wearing steel-toed boots. Architecture seemed a great fit. But strangely, my career has instead revolved around my ability to envision and construct phrases, sentences and paragraphs. This result might speak to deficiencies in design education, but the inference and conclusion are irrefutable: I've run into too many designers, artists and architects at all levels who've either forgotten or never learned the basics of stringing together words to convey clear written meaning.

I hope this book is helpful to creative people and those who help them tell their stories.

CHAPTER 1 – AUTHOR TIPS

"The reader will soon discover that these rules and principles are in the form of sharp commands, Sergeant Strunk snapping orders to his platoon."

- E. B. White, "Introduction," *The Elements of Style*, 1979 Edition

Anyone who has worked with me has heard a few favorite adages and aphorisms, as my vocabulary-obsessed father would say, ad infinitum. Here are some favorites. Each of the following tips conveys a critical bit of guidance for those selecting words and crafting phrases. Many carry over from my literary training. Logistical note: from here on, architects are included in my use of "designer."

Tip #1: You can't write the first sentence until you've written the last

While you might have an idea for an opening sentence, writing is a journey. Finding valid words, stringing them together into sentences, linking those sentences as paragraphs and molding them into a persuasive story is akin to the process of design—it's nonlinear. I remind writers not to finalize a first sentence until they lay out their entire piece of writing. We do the same in literature. Writing the first sentence before the journey of writing is complete can limit and stifle the process of discovery that makes much of what we do in life exciting and meaningful and, ultimately, limit the impact of the opening statement.

Tip #2: Murder your darlings

The idea of "killing" words and phrases we might be especially pleased with is common advice in literary circles. People get attached to words—especially phrases they have invested time and effort into honing. In the literary magazine Tin House, writer Seth Fried attributes this guidance to English writer Sir Arthur Quiller-Couch. Literary circles perpetuate the phrase to override the objectivity lost by an author's emotion, egotism and passion for a word, phrase, storyline or other fodder.

Often, the "darling" is irrelevant, doesn't belong, is ego based (has little relevance to others) or is a distraction from the larger work. Fried notes that "darlings" can be charged with biases and/or superficial interests, making them ideal literary murder victims. Be willing to edit your work. Select only the clearest examples that reinforce your piece of writing's unique message. Ditch the rest.

Tip #3: A picture is not always worth 1,000 words

The irony is not lost on me that I'll use over 550 words to explain why this advice deserves a sister phrase: "A thousand words are worth five thousand." The idea has two interpretations. First, pictures alone will not communicate the value and meaning of your work. Second, make the words you use count.

In 2005, I had the honor of being chosen to attend the Zoetrope Writers' Retreat, which is part of Francis Ford Coppola's creative network. There, I got the chance to work with the esteemed contemporary author and Booker prize winner, George Saunders.

In Saunders's first class, he passed out a 600-word story and asked everyone to cut 200 words without compromising its meaning and action. Then, a few of us read our attempts aloud, confirming the short piece had not lost its intention. Next, he asked us to slash another 200 words, reducing the story to one-third its original length. While each of us chose different words to remove, those that remained conveyed the same meaning. Saunders challenged us to overcome our fears about cutting words and to use the technique to arrive at an understanding of a key aspect of writing's essence.

This exercise still proves valuable in nearly every writing endeavor I've undertaken. The most relatable context for designers is the word count set by a publication, page limit or the space allotted for words on a page.

I typically aim for with percentages—say, remove twenty-five or thirty percent—as I work through multiple stages of word culling. Approaching the task in stages, as Saunders's method suggests, allows the writer to take multiple fresh looks at the writing and overcome the challenge of reducing it to its essence. You might ask: why is reducing so good? Two reasons:

First, George Saunders and thousands of prominent writers before him can't be wrong. In writing, less is usually more. And successive revision only makes writing better.

From E. B. White's Introduction to the 1979 edition of The Elements of Style, he noted, "When [Strunk] delivered his oration on brevity to the class, he leaned forward over his desk, grasped his coat lapels in his hands, and, in a husky, conspiratorial voice, said, 'Rule Seventeen. Omit needless words! Omit needless words! Omit needless words!'"

Second, in the words of Kurt Vonnegut, describing a speech: "No one ever wished it longer."

Most people viewing the work of designers today, sadly, resist reading. So, get to the point. Quickly.

In misguided attempts to avoid the daunting word reduction process, a few designers resort to narrow fonts or crowded font kerning (the spacing between characters in proportion to the font) or tracking (adjusting the spacing between characters uniformly) to wrestle words into a specific space or number of pages. Don't.

Standard kerning and tracking settings ensure a font's readability. Messing with spacing to crowd letters and words together also messes with legibility and your readers. The same is true for narrow fonts. My advice: be kind to your reader. Do the hard work of whittling down the words. In the writing world, fiddling with fonts or character spacing is akin to defying the laws of proportion, white space and legibility. After trying word reduction, you will discover that 1,000 well-chosen words have infinitely greater resonance than the 5,000 (or whatever length) you began with. Get chopping.

Tip #4: Differentiate yourself

In vying for a reader's attention, consider they have likely read similar accounts before, many of which sound the same. Finding the slightest differentiation can challenge the most creative mind. Even if a distinguishing characteristic exists, describing it clearly and distinctly is another matter.

As an artist or designer, to engage others in—or invite them to—your work, you must articulate that work's unique story. Are you clear about what makes your work notable? What differentiates you? What gives it meaning for others? What are your specific contributions within the broad umbrella of your chosen discipline? Have you done anything exceptional, first of its kind, groundbreaking or remarkable in some aspect? Or perhaps you did things others before you have done, but advanced that work in a unique, better, longer-lasting, more effective, more meaningful or different way. Or perhaps your viewpoint is unusual. Consider any of the aforementioned factors.

Now, imagine how that story might unfold if you reversed the order of things. Or introduced a surprise. Toss in some emotionally packed, personalized writing using your unique voice (see Tip #5 Hear your own voice) to energize and convey your point in a new way. How much more exciting would that be for a reader? And how much more memorable? Could it cause them to act or behave differently? How much more valuable and differentiating might that be for you, your work, and your purpose in writing?

Tip #5: Hear your own voice

Readers take in the written word as if it is being read aloud. An excellent test of any written content, whether a first draft or polished prose, is to listen to how it sounds. To better know the language, cadence and phrasing that makes up your voice, hear it as others would: aloud.

In the chapter titled "Point of View: The Designer's Perspective," I explain the process of posing a series of questions; interviewing (or being interviewed); transcribing the discussion; scrubbing the transcription of all the pauses, meaningless "uhs" and similar stumbling words; searching for phrasing and thinking that is unique to the individual; and extracting it for use. I do this for all professional writing. Because the process is so reliably illuminating, I also use it for personal writing.

Free voice recorders come with most phones and digital devices. Find one that works for you. Find a time and place to tackle the Q+A in one sitting. Have it transcribed. Services such as Rev.com offer fast, cheap transcriptions. Do not freak out hearing and seeing how many times you say "uh," "so," "sort of," "kind of," "I think," etc. Most of us who aren't professional speakers use these filler words. Use Microsoft Word's "Find/Replace" function (or the equivalent in whatever software you use) and remove them. In the remaining text, you will find true statements about your work and motivations, and why your work and efforts have meaning and value to others. Use these bits of narrative to tell your story.

Tip #6: Think outside the cliché

Finding a list of clichés to avoid is just an internet search away. Do it.

The problem with any cliché is it interrupts your unique voice and story. This book is about articulating your story, not some overused and typically passé phrase that has lost its impact and therefore nullifies the information, and even passion, you are attempting to convey.

Instead, consider the meaning of the cliché. Often, they can simply be deleted or replaced with simpler, higher functioning (i.e. active) words. Try rewriting what you mean by using the cliché. For example, let's take a seriously overused contemporary cliché: "Think outside the box." Always an advocate for fewer words, how about, "think differently" or, with more words, "envision a new approach"? You get the idea.

Some truly horrible clichés should be eradicated from your writing. A list appears in "Clichés and Overused Words."

Tip #7: Be open to a new order

The order in which ideas flow from your mind and onto a page may be ideal for transferring thoughts to words. But, if the goal is for others to absorb the ideas and actions presented, your work needs to follow some order. For example, journalism uses an inverted pyramid as a default structural framework, with the most important information (the Lead) first, followed by the Facts, with Background as the last element.

From Strunk's Chapter II, "Elementary Principles of Composition," here are some words of wisdom:

"[Planning] must be a deliberate prelude to writing. The first principle of composition, therefore, is to foresee or determine the shape of what is to come and pursue that shape."

Just like killing our darlings, the order of words, phrases, sentences and paragraphs has to be fluid throughout the writing process. This allows the content—the points and ideas contained within—to follow the best path to pull the reader along and make the writing's primary points. Structure is covered in the next chapter.

Tip #8: Show, don't tell

"Show the readers everything, tell them nothing."
– Ernest Hemingway

The origins of the thinking behind "show, don't tell" are attributed to Anton Chekhov in an 1886 letter he wrote to his brother Alexander, who also aspired to be a writer. In the literary world, this abbreviated version has become a catchphrase for reminding would-be writers to use sensory details and actions rather than explanation and exposition. The resulting text is more immersive for the reader, allowing them to experience and make personal connections to all that is being conveyed through the writing rather than being told.

Tip #9: Be certain, confidant and, where possible, precise

Recently when teaching a group of architects about writing, we got into a discussion about the "hedging" that happens when architects—this applies to all creative disciplines, but architects are the most egregious hedgers—speak about their work. What we are talking about here are the "sort ofs," "kind ofs," "maybes," "perhaps" and other tentative verbal couches that too readily populate much of our speaking, weaken the speaker's credibility and introduce doubt to readers and listeners. I have thoughts on this... (Of course, I do.)

The positive argument for including "approximating" terms is that they help the architect, designer or artist's language reflect the speculative, aspirational process of creation. This is the "we don't know until it's done" rationalization for speaking about what we're doing without conviction.

My counter is the "sort of," "kind of," "maybe," "I think," "I believe" and other similar phrases that pepper every interview I do with designers emerge from how we are educated. The critique and/or jury process has typically relied upon an offensive posture for jurors and a defensive one for the student being reviewed. This interpersonal dynamic, the culture of design, and the aura of intellectual pursuits intentionally establish and reward a win-lose communication dynamic and reinforce deferential behavior. Not the best climate for progress and innovation in the real world.

Mid-career architects and other creative professionals involved in education tell me this critique dynamic is fading, but many emerging designers roll their eyes and nod in acknowledgment: Oh yeah, it's still happening. Few instructors in the creative fields are teaching students how to feel empowered and confident in speaking about their work. Too many students sound like they are apologizing for having a new idea. Why? Because they were taught this behavior through their academic and practice cultures.

Perhaps creatives believe the expression of uncertainty imbues them with an aura of thoughtfulness, intellectual dexterity or designer-ly speculation. Sorry. Couching language has the opposite effect. To the public, business community and, potentially, clients and constituents, it smacks of self-focus and an absence of leadership. At the extreme, it suggests incompetence. Writers and speakers who suffer from a self-imposed overabundance of uncertainty, vulnerability and/or perceived self-doubt lose the opportunity to win audience trust and suspend disbelief—required to engage an audience in your writing or speaking. Once lost, these qualities are nearly impossible to regain. More simply stated, don't blow your chance to make a strong first impression.

The challenge is: how to empower architects and artists to speak and write with confidence about their work based on the aspirational and unknown outcomes of the creative process? Stop hedging, stop couching, stop saying "kind of," "sort of," "maybe," etc. Even "I think" and "I believe" can go beyond casual communication—these phrases can soften strong statements for some audiences—but if you are writing or formally presenting the "I think/I believe" are givens: the information is obviously coming from you.

To put this advice into action, I tested out a few well-known, powerful, aspirational phrases just to see how their sentiments and impact might change when burdened and weakened by approximation and uncertainty:

> We hold these truths to be self-evident.
> *We* **believe** *these truths* **might be** *self-evident*
>
> Love thy neighbor as thyself...
> *Love thy neighbor* **kind of** *as thyself*
>
> They lived happily ever after.
> *They lived* **sort of** *happily ever after.*

Want people to be excited about your work, your ideas and/or your creative process? Don't be speculative or fuzzy. Be excited. Be self-assured. And, when you present a fully explored idea or solution, speak or write about it with certainty. Your audience—be it a client, an emerging talent or the public—needs to feel confidence in you and the ideas you are presenting. Your words (and actions) make that confidence evident.

Tip #10: Thou shalt not bore

"I have ten commandments. The first nine are, thou shalt not bore."

– Billy Wilder, Film Director

This one should go without saying. Write to engage. Write with excitement about your work. Write with conviction and confidence. And do it effectively. But always, always, write for others.

Those with massive egos may feel empowered about the ideas floating in their heads. Remember the focus of this tip: do not bore, which also implies do not BE a bore. Typically, ego-based writing (and spoken soliloquies where one artistic voice holds the room, barely taking a breath to check in on whether the audience is still with them) is a snore to read (and listen to) because the writer/ speaker is too into their own head.

Ego-based writing and thinking doesn't technically come from an empathetic mindset interested in the ideas of others. If you find yourself mired in your head and too attached to your own ideas, see Tip #2: Murder your darlings, and then talk to others about your ideas. And next listen. Give the stuff in your head a 'test drive'. Say it aloud. Ask a friend to hear it and offer feedback. Then put the feedback to use. Don't be afraid to ask, is this even interesting?

Consider that sharing the minutia of the internal turmoil involved in your creative process may not be as interesting to your clients or audience as it was to you. It's likely they have other priorities like their own work or running an organization. To avoid boring your listeners, tailor your message. Strategize the main points to address the things your audience cares about. Ask questions or invite other voices into the story.

A related topic to Tip #9 above, be selective about the abstract, the conceptual, and the general. Favor the specific, the finite, the tangible and the real.

Be explorative during your creative process, but follow Billy Wilder's mantra, "thou shalt not bore" and use language to inspire others to understand all that creativity can produce.

Tip #11: No one ever wished it longer

Originally credited to Samuel Johnson (British writer and critic, 1709-1784) in his review of John Milton's epic poem, *Paradise Lost*, the phrase has grown to have a life of its own. What better place to extend that life than as the closing tip in this series?

Johnson reminds us we are not the only era to experience pressure for brevity. Get to the point. Have a structure and organization for your writing so one idea builds on another to reach a conclusion. Do the same for presentations and speaking. Be concise. Tell navigable stories that hit home. Those who ramble, whether writing or speaking, quickly lose their audiences. Value your audience's time and attention. Show some respect. Write and speak like you care and like it matters. Because it does.

CHAPTER 2 – WHAT READERS WANT

"Don't tell me the moon is shining; show me the glint of light on broken glass."

– Anton Chekhov

You may not think that writing for the arts, design, architecture or even business or technology involves creating stories, but it does. While you someday may write for an A.I. (Artificial Intelligence) computer or reader, for now your audience is still human. Humans become engaged with the written word through emotion.

Every reader wants a gripping story, one worthy of emotional investment. They want to build a personal connection to the material being conveyed, so they become deeply engaged, ideally to where the world around them falls away.

In fiction—and while we are not creating fiction, the genre provides valuable tips—a goal is "the suspension of disbelief." From Scientific American:

Poet Samuel Taylor Coleridge coined the term "suspension of disbelief" in 1817, but almost two centuries would lapse before we could infer how the brain might support this puzzling phenomenon. Coleridge asked readers of his fantastical poems, including The Rime of the Ancient Mariner, to give him "that willing suspension of disbelief for the moment, which constitutes poetic faith." That phrase, "poetic faith," encapsulates what our brain is doing. It isn't that we stop disbelieving—it's that we believe two inconsistent things. We accept that we are sitting and reading or watching a movie. We also believe or, more accurately, feel that what we are reading or viewing is happening.

When you write, your mission is to invite the reader to become so invested in the words that their focus intensifies, and the rest of the world disappears. Readers take in words on a page or screen as if those words are being read to them. The best way to know if your writing works is to read it aloud, or better yet, have it read aloud by someone else (or your computer). See Chapter 1, Tip #5, Hear Your Own Voice, for more.

Engaging an Audience

"Why read this?" This is the quintessential question asked by anyone seeking to understand more about your work through narrative. Writers seek an audience. But readers are busy and have their own lives to contend with. You must win them over. Other than in journals or diaries, words on a page are meant to be read by someone other than the writer. This places the onus on writers to compel readers to pick up the material to begin with, read the first page, turn that page and the next—again and again. What is the best strategy for achieving this? Give the reader what he or she needs to form an emotional attachment to the material. To engage. To suspend the disbelief or focus on their lives and businesses to turn their attention to your writing. How does this best happen? By inspiring them to care about what you are telling them on an emotional level.

Because we aren't writing fiction when writing about our design or artistic work, important aspects of the story are details about our motivations, actions, settings, challenges, results or conclusions. To see how storytelling applies in this context, let's look at the framework of the professional narrative arc.

Structuring a Narrative

Envisioning something that didn't exist and then creating it is both a mental process and a creative journey. To paraphrase thoughts on writing from this book's Foreword author, Michael LeFevre:

> *Chances are you didn't spring from the womb as a stellar designer or magically become one overnight. Your career and ascension to a point that warrants writing your story emerges from a body of results with many milestones achieved along the way. Perhaps some specific events, mentors and turning points shaped or redirected your path. Now, you will have to tell readers—whoever they may be—about that process and the result. Without lapsing into melodrama or your life's story, convey the memorable cusps in your development that might have influenced you. Conflicts, decisions, influences, redirections. These back stories add humanity and*

empathy that cement the reader's appreciation of your career focus areas. They can also create investment and belief.

We all like a good story. Stories are memorable. They are not disordered thoughts, emotions and experiences. They involve the passage of time, characters, different settings, plots, conflicts and story arcs. All conveyed with specific, credible, believable details to make them come alive and feel real. They also have climactic moments, often in the middle or toward the end. Turning parts and pieces into complete stories requires a narrative structure: a beginning, a middle and an end. These three parts come together to form the storyline or plot—the story's organizational framework. Each element must be compelling on its own—a story within a story—and play well with the other two parts to create a fully engaging and memorable piece of writing. But how and where do you begin?

Openings

"I do not see myself as a footnote to someone else's life."

– Martha Gellhorn

As a writer before becoming an architect (and a designer before becoming a writer), my preference is to hold off writing the first line of any composition until after a rough sense of the entire piece has been drafted (see "Begin at the End," below). Once a writer can see all the way through to the piece's ending, more often than not, the story has changed so significantly during the process that the most brilliantly, word-smithed opening sentence is scrapped because it no longer applies. And the writer's understanding of the meaning of their story has deepened exponentially.

Here are a few literary guidelines on the function of the words, phrases and sentences that make up an opening line or paragraph:

- Opening lines should possess most of the elements that make up the story being told.
- An opening line should have a point of view and a rudimentary statement of all that follows.
- Opening paragraphs should orient the reader to who is speaking (point of view) and time and place of the narrative.

This is the reader's first impression of your work, your approach and the ideas behind both. Opening sentences and paragraphs carry enormous weight. Make them good. Read them aloud. Repeatedly. And never hesitate to review and revise. Then, do all that again to get it exactly right.

Stories (On Borrowing)

Telling your story requires a review and honest assessment of what brought you to this moment. It demands an investigation into the motivations that drove your choices along the way, whether you are trying to tell the story of your career, a phase in your career or an individual project.

Michael LeFevre tells a story on structure that involves, in his words, "shamelessly borrowing from the best." In a keynote presentation at a building design conference, he explains how he borrowed from The Wizard of Oz for a talk on current trends in building information modeling:

> *I stole from no less than the legendary Frank L. Baum and his 1929 tale of the Wizard of Oz and subsequent film to deliver a talk on current trends in building information modeling. Part 1: Somewhere, preceded Part 2: Over, followed by Part 3: The Rainbow. In the presentation I opened with a story of personal failure, my failure to listen to a client and build a suitable physical model. My purpose in this? Building empathy and connecting with the audience through common experiences. I then covered a series of conflicts and resolutions—technical content, supporting examples and stories also known as scenes and chapters in the story—before concluding with triumph and closure: finding the rainbow that resulted from use of this new, collaboration technology.*

By borrowing from this familiar three-part narrative, Michael used a story of personal awakening that the audience could appreciate and become invested in based on their common experiences in the building industry. His use of three-part storytelling made it easy for the audience to follow the journey and to willingly suspend their disbelief. It allowed for free audience association since they were already familiar with the material. Yip Harburg's lyrics and the time-tested film have persisted for good reasons. LeFevre states:

> *Countless attendees approached me afterward to comment on some aspect of my talk that touched them because of the familiar, comprehensible, yet personal nature of the story.*

Michael successfully turned what could have been a dry technical talk into a personal story with a beginning, a middle and an end. By using this proven structure, he built trust, eased the audience's navigation, and made the story memorable.

Thousands of great story arcs and structures exist—do an internet search on story structure to glimpse a few. Kurt Vonnegut documented eight in his rejected master's thesis, "The Shapes of Stories." Freytag's Triangle (or Pyramid) is a popular standard. Borrow them. Adapt them. Make them your own. Create new ones. Strunk and White offer excellent advice on form and structure:

> *Before beginning to compose something, gauge the nature and extent of the enterprise and work from a suitable design. Design informs even the simplest structure, whether of brick and steel or of prose. You raise a pup tent from one sort of vision, a cathedral from another. This does not mean you must sit with the blueprint always in front of you, merely that you had best anticipate what you are getting into.*

Writing anything without having a plan of attack is analogous to designing a building without a floor plan or a structure in mind or a vision, medium and process for an artistic pursuit. The same goes for designing words. The structure, or order, of your storytelling will allow readers to join in your adventure of discovery more easily. More from Michael:

> *Your fellow humans, desperate for meaning and connection in our lives, will jump at the chance [to....]. Yes, your writing has this kind of potential. No matter how technical or rote the subject, almost any expository attempt is better told in the form of a story, if it can be.*
>
> – Michael Alan LeFevre, 2022

On Shape

I typically recommend a piece of professional writing, such as an article, white paper or award submission, make three overarching points composed in five parts:

1. The opening paragraph. Essentially a prelude to the three points being made, with the opening sentence providing a "hook" to engage the reader.

2. The second paragraph. Addresses the most important of three points, tackling the critical details of the points being made, with the first sentence serving as a prelude to the content of each.

3. The third paragraph. Covering the second most important content, again with the first sentence being a prelude.

4. The fourth paragraph. Encompassing the last of the three points.

5. A closing paragraph. Reiterating the main points of the opening paragraph but with the added insight, support and detail of the three central paragraphs.

Begin at the End

In T*he Seven Habits of Highly Effective People,* Stephen Covey includes a few pieces of wisdom for writing. One idea on structure is Habit 2, "Begin with the End in Mind." Ask yourself: What is your purpose? Inevitably, it falls somewhere between wanting to influence, convince, persuade, effect change, or win work. In writing, you have a purpose. A point. If not, don't bother. Often, knowing the end—the primary point you want to reveal—can inform the shape of the story. Identify the stages, steps, revelations, actions or experiences that led you to that end and use them as a framework to shape the writing.

This stepped or staged structure will help your readers understand your design, approach, value proposition, differentiators, journey, beliefs—and most importantly—what knowledge of all this might do for them. Your goal is to connect, make them want to read more, to give of their time, money and attention. Perhaps you're trying to get them to hire you, buy something you created, or trust and value you. Revisit the first part of this chapter to find what readers want and engage them.

All the while, as Covey reminds us, "The main thing is

to keep the main thing the main thing." Stick to your purpose in telling a particular story from the insight you gained from envisioning its end. In architectural parlance, as you let your site, parti, or concept vision drive the design, form, details and materials, do the same when designing words.

The Protagonist

Protagonist (noun)

- *the leading character, hero, or heroine of a drama or other literary work.*
- *a proponent for or advocate of a political cause, social program, etc.*
- *the leader or principal person in a movement, cause, etc.*
- *the first actor in ancient Greek drama, who played not only the main role...*

– dictionary.com

This primary character—you, your work or the designer you are writing for—must invite connection with readers. The character's passions must compel them to continue reading a sentence, paragraph, page or volume of pages.

Perhaps this assignment is easier if the protagonist is a person, but for those new to writing, shifting the point of view to the created object can provide a perspective-freeing exercise. I've challenged young architects to write stories in which the protagonist is a person or a building. In writing from the building's perspective and framing actions taken to achieve its vision, they consistently and effectively convey stories that transcend standard marketing writing. In this way, a building project or other endeavor can be an effective protagonist. I do the same with artists, asking "What are the work's motivations? What actions does the work take to achieve its desired result?"

The core requirement is to answer the "why care" query for your protagonist using the best tool available: emotion. Emotion creates a genuine connection for readers. How do readers find the emotion within a story? Through the actions of its main character or characters, typically the protagonist. For more on the Protagonist and a story's Point of View, see Chapter 3 – The Creative Point of View.

Action

For the purposes of story, no challenge is worthy unless the protagonist takes action to overcome it. Action is one of the most difficult narrative elements for any writer, because action demands strong, clear, active language. We all "do" things, "are" present, "see" what is happening, "listen" to what people say, hopefully, and "will do" something in the future. However, those verbs—to do, be, see, hear and propose—make for dull reading and weak stories.

The writer's challenge lies in selecting strong, active words. (See Chapter 8, "Cultivate Your Vocabulary.") Avoid passive language by using this formula to ensure an active voice:

[Subject] + [Verb (performed by Subject)] + [Object]

The object can be optional. For example, Jill [subject] + ran [verb performed by subject] creates a complete sentence:

> Jill ran.

By adding an Object, a specific destination, we create a more descriptive statement:

> Jill ran to the swimming pool.

And to not leave her hanging, let's finish the example of our character Jill from above:

> Jill dashed across the scorching pavement to plunge into the cool water of the swimming pool.

Challenge & Conflict

Every story worth telling contains conflict and challenge. Think of Moby Dick or The Old Man and the Sea. In contemporary terms, think of the forces Luke Skywalker overcame in Star Wars, the challenges Spike Lee layered into Do the Right Thing, or the massive corporate power at work against Erin Brockovich. If you must, think of Ayn Rand's The Fountainhead protagonist Howard Roark, despite his being a flawed construct for the profession. Ego and failure to serve others aside, Roark faced and overcame many challenges and is an excellent example of the importance of conflict and challenge in creating absorbing writing.

In describing his own career, one architect told me, "The architect should never be the protagonist." Why? Because empathy is a core prerequisite (over talent) to becoming a good designer. Paraphrasing the words of this insightful practitioner: at its core, design exists to serve others. And that is one secret for creating your story: practice for others and write about it for others.

Of artists, that same architect said, "Artists are protagonists because they focus on expressing themselves." This may be true, but if you, dear artist, want others to care about what you've created and are trying to express that meaning through your work, apply the "why care" principle.

The books and movies noted above are wildly successful. Why? Because they all contain protagonists who face conflict and overcome challenges. Certainly, they are extremes compared to average experience. But if you can reframe aspects of your work around the challenges and conflicts you faced in creating an outcome, resolution, design solution or artistic work, you will have a far more persuasive story than simply doing great design work. Ask yourself, if you don't believe in and can't speak to the higher meaning of your work, why should anyone else care?

In analyzing one of your projects or stories as the focus of your writing, consider: what's unique about it? Who should care? What is different, new or noteworthy, and how did it help or benefit others? What did it change? What did—or will—it achieve?

Because we are already working within the frame of challenge and conflict, a manageable assignment is finding active language to describe the actions you took to overcome a challenge or remedy a situation.

What's your objective? Perhaps you simply want to understand, focus or advance an aspect of your work, or someone else's, for everyone. Maybe you want to give back to your community. The preparation, planning and reflection required for good writing will provide new ways of thinking and seeing. The journey and discovery that brings will influence your work, your ability to mentor others, and your value as a designer to others and to society.

Introduce Others

Another mechanism for expanding action and interest is to introduce other people, or characters, your readers can connect with. For example, conflict between two characters is typically more active and engaging than an abstract soliloquy on internal conflict. What problem did you face together or in opposition to someone else? How did you overcome and rise above the challenge? Look at your colleagues, collaborators and peers as potential candidates to make your story richer, the action more relatable, and the resolution more applicable. Skip the hyperbole, love fests and brag sessions. Save them for another place and time—like one-on-one or never. Try sharing some trials and hurdles you overcame along the way. Be honest. Be humble. Vulnerably and judiciously share qualities that bring out your sincerity, humanity, approachability and, if applicable, expertise.

CHAPTER 3 – THE CREATIVE POINT OF VIEW

"Put your ear down close to your soul and listen hard."

– Anne Sexton

Establishing your voice—also known as point of view—is essential to communicating the meaning of your work to anyone, especially in written form. Finding your unique voice is essential to telling the story of your practice and work. Unfortunately, many professional and fine arts programs don't provide the communication tools necessary to speak or write about design or artistic work to the public.

My storytelling philosophy for designers defines a new fundamental for expressing the broad swath of roles and functions they and artists serve in society. Architects and designers solve problems; artists challenge beliefs and conventions. These are the protagonists in the stories we create. Thus, the protagonist's actions are essential to the story, whether it be about an object, artifact, learning experience, organization, alternative way of thinking or community, etc. The point: creating compelling stories is not about navel gazing or cataloging accomplishments for a lifetime achievement award. No, it's about conveying meaningful work so others can learn, grow or change because of that work and its success.

What is your written work's "context," physical location or larger cultural or social framework? Who are its users? What is the overarching idea, structure and concept that organizes it into a memorable whole? Apply this thinking to whatever you write: project descriptions, cover letters, specifications, design concept narratives, expert subject matter, white papers and technical work. As fellow humans, your readers will appreciate it.

Point of View: The Designer's Perspective

A primary storytelling tenet is that the perspective of the protagonist is essential to the action and outcome of the story.

One of the first questions I ask those who come to me for help in developing their narrative is, "What brought you to this career choice?" The answer to this question is the first step in developing what the literary world refers to as "point of view" (POV).

Beyond that first query, consider a series of questions to define a specific point of view around an effort, a project or an achievement. These questions focus on motivation, perspective and intention. The Q+A uncovers these forces while revealing and honing that writer's "language"—the key terms, vocabulary, speaking cadence, and favorite phrases and communication patterns that define their narrative voice. In answering these questions, look to reveal the fundamental motivations and themes in your work, or that of your client.

For an audience to become invested in your story, you must provide information that appeals to human emotion. This means you must have in mind—I'll explain the specifics of this phrasing in a moment—your passion, inspiration and personal connection to your efforts. These characteristics are not necessarily something you express directly. For example, let's say Sarah Smith has answered these questions for design:

> *Q: Why did you become a designer?*
>
> *A: "My father was a meticulous craftsperson and contractor who took me to all his jobsites. Seeing buildings being constructed inspired me to become an architect."*

While this helps us understand why Sarah became a designer, it may not be necessary or valuable in creating her story. Why? Because this bit of personal history, while of value for a memoir, essay or presentation to a class of aspiring designers, is too distant from the larger results and impact of a career or project. Instead, we might push Sarah to highlight a few distinctive details in her design work and to talk about those details. We might also ask additional questions about the craft present in her projects and ask for imagery that illustrates this area of importance to her (her POV). Our goal: to find evidence of that early passion and reinforce it in the written content and imagery for her writing. Going back to our earlier threshold: Who cares that Sarah went to jobsites? So what? What does it mean and how did it manifest itself in her work, unique story and impact on others? Ponder the events, projects, mentors, awakenings and unwavering beliefs that have driven or shaped her career – or yours in your writing.

You can also use the Q+A to reverse engineer your story starting with your reasons for undertaking an endeavor or path in your career.

Q+A Sample Questions

- What brought you to a career in design/art?
- What do you hope to accomplish most in your work?
- How do you hope to inspire others?
- Do you have a foundational philosophy? For example, what drives/has driven your creative process?
- What drives/has driven you to want to articulate what you do and what you've created to others?
- What have you been doing most recently? What are the key moments, motivations and/or initiatives that brought you to this point?
- Are there repeating patterns or themes in your work? What are they? Do they overlap or have commonalities, or is each distinctly different?

- What has brought you joy?
- What do you fight for?
- What do you inevitably turn a conversation to? What is your "soap box" topic or the idea that impassions you?
- Did you push something beyond what others thought necessary? What was that thing, and why did you push so hard? What did you hope to accomplish?
- Have you had any career milestones or epiphanies? Was there a point where your approach changed significantly, you followed an alternative path, or others felt empowered by something you did?
- Have you experienced a major life or career event or turning point where everything that followed had more direction and/or purpose?

Drill down as deeply as your mind can take you to answer the why, what, how, and what happened afterward in your work. What did you leave behind as a result and how has it changed or improved all that was there before?

Q+A How to

Tip #6, "Hear Your Own Voice," applies here. Set aside time to do the Q+A, sit down and start a voice recorder. Ask yourself the questions listed above (or better yet, have someone interview you). Answer honestly.

Have the recording transcribed. Clean it up, as noted in Tip #6, and then extract the language that genuinely speaks to you, your motivations and intentions. Copy-paste those words, phrases and sentences into a new document, perhaps even a spreadsheet for analysis, tagging and sorting. Classify, group and organize them into overriding themes and patterns.

Unearthing Themes

Many of us have needed time to discover and grow our passions—the themes of our work. This is especially the case for creative types. Under the broad umbrella of designer or artist, it's time to consider, what are your specialties, focus areas and ongoing passions? What have they been?

Unearthing themes can be tricky. There's a good chance that you haven't spent your career with a clear perspective on the rationale and motivation behind your dogged pursuits or underlying purposes. Those who have found their subtexts are lucky. Their stories will be clearer.

A theme is "a unifying idea or subject, explored via recurring patterns, or comparisons and contrasts... [the] truth at the heart of the protagonist's arc," according to K. M. Weiland, author of *Creating Character Arcs.* But how and where do you find them? To identify themes, look for and find your truth—the constants, threads, through lines, arcs or longer-term pursuits, beliefs and tenets that have guided your career.

People

Distilling the essence of your story in the quest to find themes requires self-awareness, which isn't always easy. Others can help you in this analysis—those you know through your work are excellent resources. An alternative avenue to find your themes is to ask others. What do your clients, partners, family, friends, peers—even competitors or advisors outside your discipline—think makes you tick? Ask them. Listen. Record.

Your various human connections offer a dramatic advantage: these people can see you through an external, unfettered lens. While you may pride yourself on being an empathetic consensus builder, for example, they may perceive you as an egotist hell-bent on implementing your vision. You thought you were designing schools; they saw you as a community leader and role model. And so on. To find your truth, better to ask and seek multiple inputs and versions of the truth to find what resonates.

You will find even more insight by engaging those in your field who do not know your work well. Outside perspective can bring objective insight not possible from those who know you well and most likely admire your work. I have a saying: all feedback is good, but not all feedback is valid. In other words, the insight provided by others offers intelligence for evaluating where your story works and where it may miss the mark, but it also may be superfluous.

Place & Time: Setting and Context

Another source of thematic meaning in your work is to view what you've done, and the people you've done it with and/or for, in context.

Context may offer insight into why you've followed a particular path. Did your client's concern about the health of their workforce inspire you to advocate for healthy design features in all projects? Did your neighbor lose their home because of a cutback? Did this event spur you to action to solve homelessness in your community? Did you collaborate on a project to be more inclusive as a response to lagging diversity and inclusivity and other calls for a fairer society? Look to "when, how and what" for information and motivation on your passions and behaviors.

Look for Signs

If your themes haven't yet revealed themselves, you may simply need to look deeper and ponder the results of your work. What are the repeating or recurring elements in your work? Who is your audience? To see how themes may have "shown" themselves over the years, look for signs and patterns. Know this: they're there. Keep looking until you find them.

Let Facts Speak

When writing about your work, credibility must be the

foundation. Deception or falsehoods serve no purpose—if this is what you want to write, choose fiction. The best way to make your story credible is to provide facts, results or ramifications. No amount of opinion, general praise or hearsay will convince a reader that what you are writing is worth devoting time to reading. For the rest, remember the writer's refrain: "show, don't tell" of Tip #8.

You may ask, how do you demonstrate results? One good way is with metrics. Did you or your work win acclaim? How much over the last few years? Say so. Did your work resolve or draw attention to an injustice? Show that story by saying how many people it reached and what they did in the aftermath. Did the local newspaper or trade journal feature your work and discuss its impact? Share it. Facts speak volumes. They let your readers make informed judgments for themselves, free of fluff, "marketing-speak" and babble.

Result

Inherent in developing an impactful narrative is the designer or artist providing evidence of specifics achieved in their work. In other words, no false claims. To drive this point home, I expand on this idea by asking clients to think about the beat or beats that happened after an effort was completed. They must all answer the question: what does it mean? And "meaning" here does not involve flowery prose, but a result that is measurable and witnessed, or experienced, by others who can testify to that meaning beyond a designer "doing a great job" or an artist being especially talented.

A writing-worthy result:

- Has happened because of the designer's involvement and was, ideally, not possible without that involvement.

- Influences or changes something or someone, be they peer, aspiring designer, a community, the public, an academic program or its allies, a campus or a specific group of individuals.

- Has solved a problem, overcome a challenge, added or expanded lacking systems or programs, or brought something new to the "table": a technological innovation, a product that has proven beneficial to others, or a piece of artwork or public space that provides a resolution to a social issue.

- Has been shared with others beyond the walls of your studio or office such as with peers, the public, allied agencies, government bodies and academia. A natural inclination is to ask, Why is sharing important? Because only by opening your work to the impressions and perspective of others can its value and meaning—its thematic weight—be validated.

Spin Doctors

Anyone can find a spin doctor to transform a story into a newsworthy narrative, but this isn't what resonates with readers, who seem more sensitive than ever to hyperbole, marketing-speak and being "sold" something. Social media and the rise of mis- and disinformation have exacerbated the problem and refined our skills as skeptics. Using a spin doctor to tell stories about you or your work is fine—I've benefited from the practice—but in doing so, we miss the chance to learn and grow. Better to sharpen your pencil or dust off your keyboard to wrangle your own words into a cohesive, interesting, singular story.

CHAPTER 4 – AUDIENCE

"I've learned that people will forget what you said, people will forget what you did, but people will never forget how you made them feel."

– Maya Angelou

You don't have to sacrifice or shape-shift your identity for your reader. Be who you are. Express all you've unearthed about your unique voice—your point of view. And tell the truth. (We aren't writing fiction.) Do it all in the context of your readers, out of courtesy and respect for them. Knowing your intended audience and what they care about will increase the chances of their reading your writing and gaining what you intend them to—your reason for writing in the first place. To be most effective, ask: Who is your audience? What is their style and culture? The answers to these questions are usually expressed in the reader's language, history, dress and behavior. Look, listen and care.

Who am I writing this for?

Developing an awareness of your audience provides clues to the information you should include in your writing, how it is organized and what details to include to ensure they understand and connect to what you are conveying.

For example, perhaps you are writing a grant proposal to a committee composed of bankers. Research the corporate values and culture of the organization they represent in crafting the material. The writing should be well organized and succinct—likely a linear path from point A to B to suit their bottom-line thinking. If your client is the State Board of Regents, you might discuss the power of education, students, learning, legacy and stewardship. Your writing's structure might use subheadings or themes to build your case. If you are writing for Nike, your language and style might shift to become more direct, athletic, hip, even flippant: "Just do it" in Nike's parlance. Here, your writing might be more eclectic, the structure free-flowing, perhaps following a series of challenges to crest at an emotional conclusion or celebration.

Another key audience question is Why will they read this? Are you presenting a unique perspective that adds to a larger discourse? Are they looking to hire a designer? Are they awarding grants? Selecting exhibition materials? Giving recognition? Looking to be entertained? Do they need information you have? Consider the "why" of your audience as a core part of knowing them well.

Culture

In getting to know the members of your audience, consider the expressions they use. Do they outwardly express their culture and beliefs or is their communication style more oblique? There is nothing wrong—and everything right—with slanting your writing to your audience; it's often the only way to get your message across to a group unfamiliar with you and/or your ideas. But don't be insincere. Empathy and respect should be your guides.

Writing Style

An audience should also influence the tone of your writing. To develop and present an effective argument, appeal to and address their specific conventions, vocabulary and concerns.

If your reader comes to your writing seeking information about you, your work or your expertise, your tone should be helpful and accessible. The content should be informative and actionable. Consider the task akin to sitting down with someone and sharing who you are and what you believe in and stand for.

Regardless of your reader's purpose, be vivid, know your stuff, don't mess with conventions of grammar and speech, and be yourself.

Many One True Sentences

In sharing the secret to his writing success, Ernest Hemingway said, "All you have to do is write one true sentence. Write the truest sentence that you know." These words should be your mantra. Write one true sentence about a project or endeavor. Then write another and another, so your writing is a composition of only true sentences.

Readers can sniff out fluff—it can be boring or pull them out of the story. Avoid unrelated tangents and gratuitous name-dropping. For example, you may have won a big-name award or been acknowledged by a renowned organization for an endeavor that has nothing to do with the material or story you're conveying. If so, delete it. These bits of braggadocio may cause a reader to doubt your credibility and dismiss your entire story.

Readers like to be respected. Simply put, fluff—like that 40-Under-40 award (unless your story is on the business side of your discipline) or that scouting medal—may hurt your case more than help it. Self-aggrandizement should be eliminated under Billy Wilder's rules alone: thou shall not bore. Bragging is dreadfully boring for an audience.

Let's get back to Hemingway. Whether or not you like his writing style—he was a notorious womanizer too but consider the time—think of every component of your writing as that "one true sentence." The more devoted you are to the themes or key points of your writing, the clearer and more concise your story will be, and the happier your reader.

CHAPTER 5 – WRITER TYPES

> *"Don't ever think that just because you do things differently, you're wrong."*
>
> – Gail Tsukiyama

In counseling designers about writing, I've found two types of writers:

> The Over-Writer produces a thousand words to explain a brief point and loses the reader by over-whelming them with language.
>
> The Under-Writer doesn't provide enough information for the reader to grasp the claims being made. One type of under-writer is someone who relies on images and marketing descriptions to "say it all" about a project or initiative.

The Over-Writer

The first step for an Over-Writer is to get it all out. Write your heart out. This is your instinct, after all. Your goal is to get all relevant information out of your head and onto the page. For the Over-Writer (who many of you may have identified yourself as), the mission to get from 1,000 words to 300 can be paralyzing.

Mastering the steps required to cull words is a challenge that can be overcome. Everyone who works with the allied field of graphic design to assemble and compose images and words within a limited amount of space without condensing characters knows word count limits.

Let's return to Tip #3, "A picture is not always worth a thousand words," for an exercise on reducing language. I've translated George Saunders's writing reduction exercise into simple steps for an Over-Writer to rein in verbosity:

Step 1, divide the description into 3 subsections:

- Challenge/challenges faced
- Designer's role (action/actions; what you did using strong verbs)
- Results achieved

Step 2, remove 100 words from each subsection without losing meaning

Step 3, remove another 100 words from each subsection without losing meaning

Meeting the word count allowed in the piece of writing's graphic layout is your word count goal (see "Chapter 8").

The Under-Writer

The Under-Writer often presents a greater challenge than the Over-Writer because before you can begin, you must first convince them the information provided is not enough to convey their story. The approach depends on the raw material:

- Marketing text: discard it. It's that simple. Marketing text, and even standard award text, has no place in storytelling. Such a categorical statement can be made because so much marketing writing is so bad or, in the trade's parlance, so "boilerplate". Now, doesn't that term invoke the antithesis of compelling reading?

- Over-reliance on images. Designers and artists think everything necessary can be said to everyone simply via images or observation. What's lacking story-wise in this assumption is the motivation, intention, emotion and passion behind a picture are absent. Unless you are an experienced photographer, this is rarely the case.

If you must start with an image, describe it. Describe the process of creating what appears in the image. Record yourself as you cover the basics already discussed. Use a low-cost online transcription service to hear what works.

Challenges faced? What unique obstacles slowed this project or effort? What problem were you trying to solve?

Designer's role? What did you bring to the process that

no one else could? Leadership? An approach to problem-solving? Creativity? Talent? A specialized skill? New materials or techniques? A drive to inspire social change? Or is your approach informed by nontraditional experience? If the above questions aren't sufficient, ask: if you were removed from the project or effort, would the same result be achieved? What differentiated you?

What specific actions did you take? Remember to use strong, active verbs.

What was the result? What changed? How did it change? Who benefited from the change? How far-reaching was the change?

If this Q+A results in a case of "over-writing," follow the steps in the previous section to reduce word count.

CHAPTER 6 – WHAT REBECCA RANTS ABOUT

"It's where we go, and what we do when we get there, that tells us who we really are."

– Joyce Carol Oates

I've encountered few designers who possess a complete understanding of writing fundamentals, punctuation, word choice and sentence structure. We were exposed to it in our K-12 classes, but even then, most of us didn't learn it well. If you were lucky, your professional degree program or a savvy professor might have provided some writing basics, or you attended a creative writing workshop.

Having read the writing of hundreds of designers (of all ages) and their firms' marketing departments, it seems whatever lessons were learned in school were promptly discarded upon graduation. Designers educated in alternative disciplines are usually better writers, but I won't get on my soapbox about design education in the art of communication here. In addition, the internet, social media, email and digital communications have changed the "rules of engagement" for readers, putting greater pressure on writers to say more with fewer words. We have become conditioned to being scanners and skimmers, putting exponential pressure on writing effectively and economically.

Design programs typically educate students to communicate with other design and construction professionals—the former more than the latter—and sophisticated purveyors of design. Artists less so, as they often deal with subjects outside the arts and potential buyers. With a pressing need to get the stories of designers and architects out to the public, or an unfamiliar yet discerning audience such as a jury, a fresh take on the fundamentals of writing, narrative and storytelling is essential. These conventions are invaluable to good professional writing for all audiences, including your peers.

Redundancy

To write cleanly is to eliminate redundancy, which is the use of two or more words when one could do. Here's a partial list of redundant phrases to look for and eliminate:

Redundant Word List

REDUNDANT / NON-REDUNDANT

a total of X (a number) / X (a number)

appear to be / appear

circle around / circle

close proximity / close (or in proximity)

collaborated together / collaborated

completely finished / finished

each and every / each

each separate (thing) / each (thing)

end result / result

exactly the same/the exact same / the same

free gift / gift

green in color / green

many different (things) / many (things)

new innovations / innovations

one and the same / the same

repeat again / repeat

revert back / revert

she/he is a person who is / she/he is

shorter/longer in length / shorter/longer

summarize briefly / summarize

tall skyscraper/tall tower / skyscraper/tower

Wordiness

A second, ever-present objective is to make your writing accessible and approachable to readers. One simple method is to eliminate wordiness: extra, sometimes redundant, unnecessary or empty words to express something easily stated with less language. Remember, the more words used to express an idea, the more work the reader must do to understand that idea. Jettisoning wordiness is a simple process, because many "wordy" phrases are easily searched for within a text and removed:

WORDY / NON-WORDY CHART

as to whether / whether

at the same times as / while

at this point in time / at this time/now

due to the fact that / because

for the purpose of / for

had an effect on / influenced

has to be / must be

in order to / to

in spite of the fact that / although

in the event of / if

the reason... is because / because

until such time as / until

with the possible exception of / except

Real World Wordiness

The following pages identify common redundant, awkward and wordy phrasing using examples pulled from publicly available readers' comments and award submissions. No source citations are given here because, since they lacked a background in writing and language development, we hold these folks blameless. I altered names and specifics to protect the writers' identities.

"In Order To"

The popular phrase "in order to" (equally wordy and legalese) is used frequently to make the preposition "to" loftier; however, "to" has no lofty aspirations. It's a preposition. Its job is to direct us to stronger, more active words.

Technically, prepositions function as modifiers of verbs, nouns or adjectives that express a spatial, temporal, or other relationship; for example, in, on, by, to and since. With the mission to reduce unnecessary language, "to" does the work of "in order to" with a fraction of the characters.

Examples:

"Wordy" Original

> This critical proposal prioritized the region's sustainability targets and led local and regional governments to re-think relevant planning and infrastructure stan-

dards in order to realize these goals.

"Clean" Revision

This critical proposal prioritized the region's sustainability targets and led local and regional governments to re-think relevant planning and infrastructure standards to realize these goals.

"Wordy" Original

In order to create a community where students could feel at home in this large institution, the building was broken into two academic houses, split by a daylit concourse.

"Clean" Revision

To create a community where students could feel at home in this large institution, the building was broken into two academic houses, split by a daylit concourse.

The Subliminal Negative

No phrase is more prevalent in designers' writing, and especially architects', than "not only, but." I call this viral colloquialism the "subliminal negative."

Coming to the profession after a successful career in research and development for a Fortune 500 company, where I dealt with many other well-established companies, institutions and organizations, I can confidently say this phrasing does not proliferate in language outside the profession as it does within. The reason: negative words, such as "not" and "but" (which Dictionary.com states are "used to introduce a phrase or clause contrasting with what has already been mentioned"—the key word being "contrasting") set the stage for the reader to expect negative information. Why use negative phrasing when positive words will do?

The subliminal negative, with its non-positive connotations, disinvites people to read about your accomplishments. It's like the person who begins every response with "no" or "but." "Both" is a more positive word with "and" connecting two things—"both X and Y"—providing a positive alternative to the "not only... but" statement. Technically even the term "both" is redundant if the author lists two elements after a verb, the reader can be trusted to assume that "both" is intended. If I accomplish anything with this book, advancing awareness and reducing use of "not only... but" would be a victory.

Here are some examples pulled from actual designers' writing. Note how minor changes reduce words and clarify what is being expressed:

Original "Negative" Version

> We buck the trend of traditional designer offices in terms of studio demographics with more than half of our studio members made up of women and minorities. This diversity not only defines our culture but strengthens it.

"Positive" Revision

> *We buck the trend of traditional designer offices in studio demographics with more than half of our studio members made up of women and minorities. This diversity defines and strengthens our culture.*

Original "Negative" Version

> This firm's most tangible contributions are its buildings, noteworthy not only individually but also as a body of work that is reshaping our understanding of what it means for a design to be of its time and place.

"Positive" Revision

> *This firm's most tangible contributions are its buildings, noteworthy individually and as a body of work reshaping our understanding of what it means for design to be of its time and place.*

Egregious Subliminal Negative Use

A one-page reference letter by a highly respected designer includes no less than five instances of the subliminal negative, deserving of nomination to the Subliminal Negative Hall of Fame:

Negative Original (1)

> The firm has been able to not only create a significant practice in such a place, but to also become a "citizen" designer practice, taking responsibility not

only as designers, but as citizen leaders for the evolving identity of the new [city name].

Positive Revision

The firm has created a significant practice in such a place, becoming a "citizen" practice, taking responsibility as designers and leaders for the evolving identity of the new [city name].

Negative Original (2)

The firm's schools, churches and museums fulfill not only their primary mission but also act as compelling settings for social interaction.

Positive Revision

The firm's schools, churches and museums fulfill their primary mission and act as compelling settings for social interaction.

Negative Original (3)

Their work critically responds not only to the landscape, climate and traditional building forms but also to the creation of a site fused with designer.

Positive Revision

Their work critically responds to the landscape, climate and traditional building forms while also creating a site fused with designer.

Negative Original (4)

The firm not only creates community through the social interaction their designs foster, but also through engaged community leadership.

Positive Revision

The firm creates community through the social interaction their designs foster and through engaged community leadership.

Negative Original (5)

Not only do their buildings inspire us, but their active civic leadership provides a model for an engaged urban practice.

Positive Revision

Their buildings inspire us, and their active civic leadership provides a model for an engaged urban practice.

It was/It is & There was/There is

Using a generic pronoun and verb such as "it was" and "there are" is indirect passive phrasing. In this language, the sentence's subject is acted on by something (whatever "it" is) and the true subject tends to be buried later in the sentence. Similarly, verbs such as "was" and "is" present an opportunity to replace generic phrasing with more active language.

Our goal in professional writing is to use active language, not passive. Restated, to practice what I preach: use active language as a goal. Use your "Find and Replace" function to remove these phrases and replace them with stronger, more direct language. The simple active language formula is:

Subject + Verb + Object.

Examples:

Passive/Inactive

> Informed about the parishioners' preferences, the designers devised an elegant solution for the building. It was an opportunity to bring a diverse community together behind a single vision.

Active

> *Informed about the parishioners' preferences, the designers identified an opportunity to bring a diverse community together behind a single vision and devised an elegant building solution.*

Passive/Inactive

> "It seemed to me that the Design Review Board was kind of a broken model, so I got involved with the city's Get Engaged program and joined the Design Review Board."

Active

I recognized the Design Review Board as a broken model, so I became involved with the city's Get Engaged program and joined the Design Review Board.

Passive/Inactive

It was easy for me to verify the firm's reputation as a workplace invested in junior members' growth.

Active

I easily verified the firm's reputation as a workplace invested in junior members' growth.

Passive/Inactive

The project was completed before the adoption of LEED but recent post-occupancy monitoring of energy consumption has yielded a measured EUI of 185kBtu/sf/yr. (50% below benchmark), placing the project significantly below the 2030 Commitment at the time it was designed and constructed.

Active

Completed before the adoption of LEED, recent post-occupancy monitoring of energy consumption yielded a measured EUI of 185kBtu/sf/yr. (50% below benchmark), placing the project significantly below the 2030 Commitment.

Other Weak Verbs

Am / Is / Are

Be / Being / Been

Can / Could

Do / Does / Did

Has / Have / Had

May / Might / Must

Should / Shall (auxiliary verb, present singular)

Would / Will (auxiliary verb, present singular)

Was / Were

That

"That" is one of the most overused words in any writing and a prime target for reducing word count. I recently struck ninety-five percent of the uses of "that" from a client's writing (50+ words in a 1,000-word piece), significant space in a space-constrained graphic layout where every character counts.

Many, many resources exist on how and when to use "that"—too many to cover in this volume. For clean language, determine if "that" can be removed without changing the meaning of a sentence. Let's look at some guidelines. And remember, "that" for things; "who" for people.

Noun or Adjective Complement

Use "That" in a clause as a complement to a noun or an adjective to give additional information about the noun or adjective. It answers the question "why."

Examples:

> I'm frustrated that my boss always wants me to work overtime.
>
> Maggie appreciates all the work that led to project funding.

That versus Which

A debate rages between language experts on whether to use "that" and "which" to connect two sentence clauses. I found simple guidance from David the Grammarian at the Khan Academy in using these words in a sentence:

> "That" doesn't work well after a comma or in a comma enclosed clause.
>
> "Which" doesn't work well with people.

That as a Determiner

That/those used at the beginning of spoken sentences indicates an object or person—emphasis on the word "spoken." This use is better saved for casual conversations because their generic subject/object can become unclear. It's better and clearer to name the object being referred to.

Examples:

That's my sister Sara over there.

That's a book you have in your hand.

Those sculptures are by Henry Moore.

That is her house on the corner.

Expendable Uses of That

If you can remove "that" from a sentence and not lose the sentence's original meaning, then "that" is expendable and should be deleted.

Examples:

We knew that Clarence would need to hurry up.

We knew Clarence would need to hurry.

The designer suggested that the bathroom have a window.

The designer suggested the bathroom have a window.

The fact that ...

Using "the fact that..." to introduce a sentence is a filler phrase and should be deleted for brevity and clarity.

Examples:

The fact that the show was so well attended should make you giddy.

You should be giddy about the high show attendance.

The fact that Elie passed the test proves he studied hard.

Elie studied hard and passed the test.

After Reporting Verbs

Margo said (that) she must have dinner.

Coltrane told me (that) I had egg on my face.

My boss implied (that) the restaurant would soon become a nightclub.

After Adjectives

I'm happy (that) Erin got engaged.

He's sad (that) he's moving out west.

As Object in Relative Clauses

We invited the neighbor (that) I met on a walk.

Sammie wants to see the movie (that) you recommended.

Below is an example of how "that" can be removed and the wording revised to create clearer prose.

Example:

Original

> When looking to support the growing fleet of the Blue Line, this facility aims to be one of the first buildings in the area that is more urban, pedestrian friendly and progressive.

Clean

> *When looking to support the growing fleet of the Blue Line, this facility aims to be one of the area's first buildings to be more urban, pedestrian friendly and progressive.*

Cleaner

> *When looking to support the growing Blue Line fleet, this facility aims to be among the area's first more urban, pedestrian-friendly and progressive buildings.*

Awkward Obsolete Words

Sometimes we encounter writing that seems stuck in the late 19th century. No one can be certain why some writers are attracted to awkward, archaic language. Best to send these phrases to the dust pile, where they've rested happily for decades:

Not "utilize," "use" (though I'm guilty)

Not "amidst," "amid"

Not "whilst," "while"

Not "heretofore," "until now"

"Orphaned" Pronouns

To help a reader stay with you and understand the meaning you intend, re-read your work and look for "orphaned pronouns." This mean pronouns and references—for example, their, them, it, our, etc.—that have become detached from their contexts, "parents," or the sentence's subject. For example, "it" is one low functioning pronoun to look for to minimize ambiguity. Help the reader understand what you mean by "it" by being specific.

An old comedy device might come in handy. Consider Abbott and Costello's famous routine: Who's on First—a classic parody of orphaned pronouns. Ask yourself: Who's on first? What's his name? Whose name? Where is that happening? What is happening? And so on.

Repeat the object you're referring to if the phrasing relies too much on pronouns. A writing teacher once advised that a piece of prose had to state something three times before it stuck in the reader's mind. (And the guideline is for short prose.) Your reader will appreciate not getting lost or being expected to read previous material for orientation. Your job is to help them.

Biased Language

Certain words and phrases are inherently biased, often because of their origins. Many online resources are available to help you extricate biased and culturally outdated language from your vocabulary (the process is also called "decolonizing language"). I highly recommend you search them out. These lists contain many terms that should never appear in contemporary writing along with recommended alternatives. On gender, or the "he/his/him" and "she/hers/her" issue, they/their/theirs saves a lot of uses of "/". Since we are interested in eliminating extraneous characters, know your preference and be consistent.

BIASED / ALTERNATIVE WORD CHART

chairman / chair, chairperson

common man / average person, ordinary people

councilman / council member

craftsmanship / craft

grandfathered / legacy

guys / people, team

handicap / disability

man-hours / staff-hours, work hours

mankind / humanity, people, human beings, humankind

manmade / synthetic, manufactured, machine-made

workmanship / craft

craftsman / artisan

Racist, Sexist, Ableist, Xenophobic & Generally Stupid Clichés

This may seem overkill considering the current times, but where's the harm in reminding us to think again about the words we use and how they might land on the ears of others. Thankfully, the English language has more than 171,000 words in current use (more if we mine archaic language). Plenty of alternatives are available. Consider the challenge a great opportunity to expand your vocabulary.

Many more unacceptable phrases exist than are listed here. Compiling and including them felt like its own violation. I wish they were already eradicated from use, so I didn't have to repeat them below.

-IST WORD CHART

Black sheep (origins in slavery)

Blackball (racialized)

Blacklist (origins in slavery)

Blacklist/whitelist (racialized tech terms)

Blackmark (racialized)

Blindsided/blind-spot (ableist)

Bubbly (sexist)

Cakewalk (origins in slavery)

Ditsy (sexist)

Drink the Kool-Aid (use your imagination)

Dumb (ableist)

Feisty (sexist)

Ghetto (elitist)

Grandfathered/grandfather clause (origins in slavery)

Guru (cultural appropriation)

Gypped (slur)

Hip hip hooray (origins in Nazi Germany)

Hysterical (sexist)

Indian (unless related to India, the country)

Lame (ableist)

Long time no see (mockery)

Low hanging fruit (think Billie Holiday's rendition of Milt Raskin's "Strange Fruit")

Master (for space or anything)

Moron (origins in eugenics)

Mumbo jumbo (look it up)

No can do (mockery)

Nonwhite (as if "white" is the norm!)

Oriental (dehumanizing)

Peanut Gallery (segregationist)

Perky (sexist)

Savage/Squaw (N-words for Native Americans)

Sold down the river (use your imagination)

Spooky (WWII racism)

Thug (racialized)

Third world/first world (elitist)

Tipping point (origins in white flight)

Uppity (origins in slavery)

Accessible Language

Our contemporary world demands accessibility, especially in the United States since the Americans with Disabilities Act was signed into law in 1990. The design of our buildings across the spectrum from new construction to adaptive reuse and historic renovation must remedy impediments to building access for people of all abilities.

As we seek to expand awareness of the work and value of designers to society, the "archi-speak," jargon and insular communication skills you've learned as a designer are a barrier to that goal. Pun intended. The more that creative people can realign their understanding of how to craft, structure, build and refine a professional narrative, the better our chance of letting the public know who we are, what we do, and why both are important.

Embrace Writing Clean

The more unnecessary language we use, the less space we have available for language loaded with power and meaning. Writing cleanly:

- Enables faster reader comprehension
- Lower word count = more white space per page
- Lower word count = clearer hierarchy and more space for images
- Appeals to a broader audience not trained in art-speak, archi-babble, designer-ese, such as the public, users and clients
- Avoids the trap of "legalese"; technical contract language is overkill in professional communication and cumbersome for storytelling. Confine it to legal communications.
- Appeals to a tweet-conditioned audience geared to digesting limited characters

CHAPTER 7 – RULES OF ENGAGEMENT

"Our histories cling to us. We are shaped by where we come from."

- Chimamanda Ngozi Adichie

Let's be realistic. Everyone needs to recognize that the use of a comma, colon, semicolon and hyphen is not subjective or based on personal preference or style. Stop using these forms of punctuation subjectively. Punctuation marks are the traffic signals of reading. They tell us when to pause, stop, or continue and when words or phrases need emphasis. As our "rules of the road," they govern our reading and writing behavior. Academic clients in particular will be gratified to see that you learned the rules rather than creating your own and discounting their lifeblood.

Just as specifications exist for construction and material use, "specification" books and online resources exist for punctuation, grammar, word use and other aspects of the writing craft. Different style protocols exist, *The AP Style Book* (Associated Press) and *The Chicago Manual of Style* (CMS) predominating. I use *The Chicago Manual of Style* because the literary world favors it, which means it suits storytelling, while AP is for journalism by default.

Everyone has an opinion or a preference on the rules and guidelines governing punctuation. To pay homage to some empty language from my father, "the long and short of it" is that designers need to learn to tell their stories. Save the journalism for industry publications. That is my "two cents." Regardless of your preference, pick a style, understand the grammatical and punctuation conventions you make based on that style, and stick to them.

I have a few personal biases regarding punctuation in written content for awards, which you may have already noticed. Let's share. These have to do with white space and graphics:

- The more characters we place before a reader, the more characters they have to absorb.

- The more gaps that occur between words and punctuation marks, the further their eyes must travel across the entirety of a document. Bridging gaps is tiresome.

If you are truly interested in developing and presenting a comprehensive professional narrative, consider the following guidelines nonnegotiable. Apparently, these statements have started arguments among colleagues (with specification writers being especially sensitive). Don't start a war but try to embrace these principles for your writing.

Serial or Oxford Comma

This debate rages among word nerds worldwide. Plainly, it's an extra character. An extra black mark for your reader to take in. Don't use Oxford commas unless required for clarity, such as in a list of complex phrases.

Examples:

> **With serial comma:** Al received the 2010 Doris B. Turner Award and was nominated jointly by the AIA, ACEC, and ASLA for excellence in service to the built environment.
>
> **No serial comma:** Al received the 2010 Doris B. Turner Award and was nominated jointly by the AIA, ACEC and ASLA for excellence in service to the built environment.

Honestly, do you miss it? Unlike some writing, we have a confined purpose and an educated audience. Thus, more than likely, the comma here—in a simple list—is unnecessary clutter.

Remember: use the serial comma ONLY if your list is simple such as a simple list of nouns or verbs.

If you'd like to know more, Google the TED Talk on the Oxford comma. Who knew such a small bit of punctuation could be so controversial? Now you do.

Dashes

First, use the right one. Know the difference between a hyphen, em dash and en dash:

Hyphen a.k.a. A Simple Dash

Shortest of the three. Used for:

- Compound words (three-story, 10,000-square-foot building)
- To separate numbers (phone: 1-800-555-1212; Social Security: 000-00-0000)
- No spaces before or after

Exception: hanging hyphen (example: "nineteenth- and twentieth-century literature"), which has space after.

En Dash

Equals "through"; longer than a hyphen, not as long as an em dash. Most commonly indicates inclusive dates and numbers:

- 1919–1920
- July 9–August 17
- pp. 37–59

No spaces before or after, though Microsoft Word

automatically puts spaces around en dashes. The default is puzzling, and I have to remove them from many date ranges on resumes and CVs.

Em Dash

Longer than all other dashes—like that:

- Used for dash within a sentence
- Creates strong break in sentence structure
- Can replace comma
- No spaces before or after

Examples:

- Used in pairs like parentheses—that is, to enclose a word, a phrase, or a clause—or they can be used alone.
- Alone, they detach one end of a sentence from the main body—perhaps to make a strong point.

If you haven't noticed, the above statements are both instructive and models for em dash use.

Semicolon

Use 1: To separate two independent clauses NOT joined by conjunction:

Examples:

- *Comma + Conjunction:* The selected firm hails from Little Rock, Arkansas, and the Denver firm came in a close second.
- *Semicolon:* The selected firm hails from Little Rock, Arkansas; the Denver firm came in a close second.

Use 2: Join two independent clauses, use a semicolon before the adverbs:

however

therefore

indeed

besides

nevertheless

Example:

The selected firm hails from Little Rock, Arkansas; however, the Denver firm came in a close second.

The selected firm hails from Little Rock, Arkansas; therefore, the Denver firm came in a close second.

Use 3: In a list that includes commas for things such as credentials.

Example:

The team consisted of Max Smith, [credential]; Sue Jones, ASLA; and Bob Brown, [credential].

CHAPTER 8 – VOCABULARY

Never find out when you can discover.

Words are powerful. And English has more of them to play with than any other language. While phrases like "find out" work well in casual dialog, to engage readers and wrap them into a world, we need better, stronger words packed with meaning such as "discover."

My father obsessed over vocabulary. He read the dictionary every day and regularly deployed his newly acquired words on his kids. I didn't know what was happening at the time, but now I recognize he taught me the value of having a superior satchel of words at the ready—in this case, more is more.

Cultivate Your Vocabulary

Good writing demands that authors cultivate their vocabulary. This is easier today thanks to the ability to check synonyms in word processor software, via free online thesauruses, and thanks to new writing add-ons such as Grammarly, ProwritingAid and the Editor function in Microsoft Word. More options are proliferating faster than it's possible to Google "writing tools." Such resources even allow you to click through synonyms to find more variations or specific, appropriate or explanatory alternatives.

In Chapter 6, we touched on "it is"/ "it was" and "there is"/ "there was." These "to be" verbs typically offer readers nothing about the specific action involved in doing something. They are, in the realm of vocabulary, relatively uninformative. See the section below titled "State of Being Verbs."

When composing a piece of writing or any professional communication, choose words that clarify and enhance meaning. Don't overreach with obscure words—this will distance a reader—but a powerful, meaning-packed vocabulary will enthrall your reader with the story being presented and pull them along.

I often hear people lament that a designer or artist doesn't have the charisma needed to appeal to clients or patrons. A firm command of language and vocabulary can overcome this with a bit of confidence-building. Contrary to popular opinion, an MIT study says it can be learned.

Marketing Speak

Avoid marketing-speak in writing for anything other than materials used to pursue project work. (I could rant further about how the language is inappropriate for particular clients and projects.) Clients who receive marketing materials appreciate when you use sincere, specific language, rather than trying to sell them with hyperbole and clichés. Still, many designers lapse into using boilerplate or stock phrasing for explaining their careers and work to others.

Don't just avoid marketing-speak, banish it. Obliterate it. A reader is not "buying" your services. Instead, they are attempting to grasp what is unique about you and your work. Help them. Tell them plainly and simply.

State of Being Verbs

A state-of-being verb does not represent action, thought, intention or sensation. To put it plainly, these verbs are static, "to be" or "not to be." They also make for dull reading. If used in and around more active language, they result in wordiness. As noted in Chapter 6, we work to eliminate the "it was" and "there is" forms from writing to entice readers more directly with the story being told. Often, "is," "was," and their cousins like "have" are part of passive language, which is where the subject of a statement receives the action or has something done to it. Thus, the subject comes after the action.

Example

Passive

The design was done by Simone.

Active

Simone completed the design.

Chapter 6 has many more examples. While passive language is technically correct, and is sometimes necessary, our goal is to replace these sluggish verbs with more active language if we want to engage readers.

Empty Words

Many designers (and non-designers) believe using more words and multi-syllabic words make them sound smarter. They are unequivocally wrong. True brilliance, at least to write for a broad audience, is clear when a writer accomplishes much with as few—and as simple—words as possible.

Empty words are those that add nothing to a sentence. Remove them and the statement being made is unchanged. Most often, the culprit is adverbs—words ending in "ly." Eliminate these in your writing:

Actually

Apparently

Basically

Essentially

Extremely

Extremely critical *(if it's critical, its extreme by definition)*

Generally

Really

Relentlessly

Truly

Various

Very

Virtually

Empty and Filler Phrases

A compound problem is when empty words appear with wordiness to make empty phrases. Use "find and replace" to seek and destroy as to remove as many of these chronic, dull filler phrases as possible in your writing:

Again

As already stated

For all intents and purposes

Having said that

I believe*

I cannot overstate the importance of (then don't...)

I feel*

I think*

In my opinion*

In some ways

Tend to

The fact that

*If you are the author, these phrases are redundant

because your words are already expressing your ideas, thoughts, feelings, beliefs, etc.

Be kind to your reader. Search your work for other low-functioning generic, non-specific words like "sometime," "something" or "someone." Use the same exercise for the "any-" words.

Eradicate marketing-speak, redundancies, filler phrases and empty language, and renegotiate these words and phrases in deference to greater specificity and succinct, meaningful written content.

Clichés and Overused Words

In reviewing language from hundreds of design firms across the country and internationally, certain words and phrases are overused, cliched and meaningless. An example is "engage"—noble word—but any word or phrase used to excess loses its meaning for the reader.

I often imagine myself as a client having to suffer through reading a stack of proposals in which every firm says, "we engage clients and users," or "we are true collaborators." These are common phrases in professional parlance and often appear multiple times within a piece of writing. The result: reader fatigue.

Listed below is a sampling of overused words and expressions by designers and their firms. Minimize their use. Save them for when and where they have meaning. Avoid repeats. Find stronger alternate words:

Appropriate

Building

Collaborate/collaborative

Engage

Great

Good

Guide/guidelines

Holistic

Help facilitate (redundant)

Impact

Innovate/innovative

Inspire/inspiring

Integrate

Lead/leaders

Listen/listeners

Project, of the project, your project *("your" being redundant; what else would you be referring to?)*

Process *(which sounds like an arduous, dull experience. Be specific.)*

Program

Strategy/strategize/strategist

State-of-the-art

I challenge everyone writing about their actions to dig deeper. When you write, think about the over-prevalence of these words in designer lingo:

"Engage." "Interact" might better describe activities of a process of engagement; "energize" could suggest the result of the engagement process. "Immerse" and "involve" might allow your description to stand out above other engagers.

"Collaborate" can become "cooperate," "coproduce," or "partner" as one-word options, while "work together," "work side-by-side," and "come together" provide more specific phrasing to prevent overuse within a passage or paragraph.

Don't rely on these ubiquitous words and phrases if you have a choice. Say things differently. Paraphrasing countless brilliant authors: if you've seen it written on one page already, don't use it again.

CHAPTER 9 – AESTHETICS COUNT

"In my career, I've learned that if you build something beautiful, people will respect it."

– Phil Freelon, FAIA

How can we not talk about aesthetics in writing for and by designers?

Page Hierarchy

While designers and artists are well versed in the hierarchical order of spaces and elements, such as components of a façade, functions in a program, or the aesthetics of proportion and placement, they often seem challenged when asked to arrange images, graphics and text in hierarchical order on a page. (They will never admit this….) The Internet, websites, mobile devices and digital formatting have honed readers' expectations on how to sort through images and words on a page.

Readers of all languages start at the top left-hand corner of a website and move right and down as they traverse page content. Since most written content (books, articles, white papers, artist's statements, bio, outreach messaging, blogs) are now viewed digitally, a format or fundamental framework should be a consideration in layout design.

Now that you know this, use it to illuminate how you might organize, control or break your content's hierarchical flow to draw readers' eyes and attention to the information you want them to see first.

Be Consistent

- Limit number of fonts and font styles used.
- Use a generally accepted citation format.
- Punctuation: pick one punctuation guide; stick with it.
- Write out numbers or use numerals, not both.

Content

- Lists: can simplify information and make comprehension efficient.
- Diagrams, images and photographs: aesthetics count, clarity counts (avoid low-resolution), beauty counts.
- Provide sufficient white space around images and important blocks of text. Consider the most important information on a page and give it the space and scale it needs.

White Space in Writing

We have finally arrived at the point where I insist on the elimination of placing double spaces between sentences—younger readers can skip this section because putting double spaces between sentences is a dying habit. (Fingers crossed on my end.) Those who continue might say, "Enough!" Before you do, print a page of writing that has two (and sometimes many more) spaces between sentences. Then, remove the double spacing (in Word or InDesign, go to Find/Replace, punch in two spaces for "Find" and one space for "Replace," and then hit "Find all" until that number is zero).

Print the new page and pin up the two options side-by-side. Notice the lack of gaps in the one-space-between writing. Also notice the characters used less space on the page, meaning more white space to add images or allow the reader to rest.

Other notes on gaining white space:

- Add paragraph breaks. The shorter the paragraph, the more digestible the content.
- Use short headings or titles to help orient readers. Use white space between headings and the lines of text that surround them.
- Use default or automatic settings for line spacing or make the spacing larger. Never condense line spacing.

Margins and White Space

Any good designer knows the value of context—the figure ground relationship. Margins and white space in a layout offer readers space to rest. To use the old Coca Cola tagline, margins and white space are "the pause that refreshes."

Now, having gained white space by eliminating double spacing between sentences, let's also place white space around the language for a better reader experience. As we do in buildings and works of art, let's compose our work:

- Generous margins. While images look fabulous in full-bleed, text does not. Even a one-quarter-inch side, top and bottom margin is too narrow. Use one-half-inch or larger. Literary submissions require one inch all around.
- A more generous lower margin is aesthetically comfortable for readers, so use more space there if you can.
- Readers are also comfortable reading lines of text that max out at about five inches long—the equivalent of about 75-character spaces or 10 or so words per line depending on your font size.
- Use a minimum one-quarter inch spacing between columns.

Google the topic of white space and you'll find all kinds of resources, including formulas for determining the ideal length based on font size. But it's not necessary to get so technical. Just keep in mind that long lines of text are fatiguing and disorienting for readers, as are column widths that are too short (about 40 characters is optimal). Captions can be shorter (12-15 characters). As you lay out your work, remember to be kind to your readers.

Narrow or Condensed By Any Other Name

From my first moments in the field of design, I noticed an odd quirk that lurks in the shadows of professional writing and presentations today: narrow fonts.

Aside from trying to cheat or game spatial limits, narrow fonts increase the density of the content being presented and reduce its legibility. By compressing character spacing, as is done with narrow fonts, the standard format of a font is crowded. This challenges the reader to digest more content in a given space.

Narrow fonts are not found in literature because the focus is on legibility and reader comfort. As a parallel, imagine replacing all 36-inch-wide corridors in your home with 30-inch-wide ones. You'd feel that six-inch loss of space, right? When you use a narrow font or condense character spacing, you're giving your readers a similar experience.

CHAPTER 10 – THE ART OF EDITING

Editing is an art. Embrace and nurture that idea. As you approach the written word with this in mind, your ability to communicate will improve exponentially.

This book, and my practice, is fundamentally about editing—in written and graphic form—to tell better stories about designers and artists and their work and intentions. I've sought to answer many questions received over the years on what does and does not belong in professional communications and to offer advice on formatting written materials.

The Practice of Editing

> *It doesn't matter how good you think you are as a writer–the first words you put on the page are a first daft. Writing is thinking: It's rare that you'll know exactly what you're going to say before you say it.*
>
> – Harry Guinness, "How to Edit Your Own Writing," The New York Times, April 7, 2020 (Updated April 10, 2020)

You would do well to read Guinness's article. The web is also filled with videos on how to approach editing and apps to aid the process. If these appeal to you, especially as first pass editing tools, I recommend finding one that suits your needs. But an app or add-on should never be your only editing tool. Without knowledge of the rules behind these programs, I've seen writers pump out some awful prose. This book outlines tested strategies and recommendations to avoid writing problems in the first place. Then comes the most important lesson in the art of editing, which bears repeating. Forgive the redundancy in what follows:

After a first draft, read the writing aloud or have your computer read it. Do this a few times as necessary to get the content to sound correct. Each review may reveal some other flaw—an overused word, faulty syntax, a missing article or preposition. The first time I was asked to read a piece of my writing aloud (at a writers' retreat in Tepotzlan, Mexico), I read the 2,000-word piece and reread and reread it again (and again). The director of the retreat had asked that I get the reading as close to ten minutes as possible, the fewer minutes the better. I was astounded how each rereading (aloud) revealed yet another unnecessary word, phrase or sentence. This experience was a precursor to the George Saunders method shared in Chapter 1. Both approaches yielded the same result: better writing and a more satisfied audience.

Never discount the artistry of editing. Many first-time writers believe that creativity comes in the writing itself, but established authors recognize that the true artistry and magic emerges in the editing. Whatever your writing project, leave yourself time to write and revise. Set the piece aside so you can return with fresh eyes. Revise again, edit down, contemplate and read it again. Like de-cluttering your attic, your work, your mind and those of your readers will be better off with less.

Have others read the work as well. The more eyes the better. The more insight the better. Here's an odd phenomenon: as we write and revise, the brain fills in or skips over missing words and redundancies. Our brain is so attuned to what we want to say, it can deceive us. Counteracting this deception requires focus and an openness to feedback from others.

Editing Inspiration

Here are some words of inspiration on editing from those who have mastered its art:

> *"Kill your darlings, kill your darlings, even when it breaks your egocentric little scribbler's heart, kill your darlings."*
>
> – Stephen King

> *"The idea is to write it so that people hear it and it slides through the brain and goes straight to the heart."*
>
> – Maya Angelou

> *"I'm all for scissors. I believe more in scissors than I do in the pencil."*
>
> – Truman Capote

"...the secret of good writing is to cut it back, pare it down, winnow, chop, hack, prune and trim, remove every superfluous word, compress, compress, compress..."

– Nick Hornby

"I've found the best way to revise your own work is to pretend that somebody else wrote it and then to rip the living shit out of it."

– Don Roff

"The writer who breeds more words than he needs, is making a chore for the reader who reads."

– Dr. Seuss (yes, but it's still good advice)

"Not a wasted word. This has been a main point to my literary thinking in life."

– Hunter S. Thompson

"Never use a long word where a short one will do. If it is possible to cut a word out, always cut it out."

– George Orwell

"The first draft of everything is shit."

– Ernest Hemingway

Journey & Destination

"There is no greater agony than bearing an untold story inside you."

—Maya Angelou, *I Know Why the Caged Bird Sings*

The end is always a beginning

In these pages we have examined the possibility of self-discovery, outlined rules for good writing and editing, and delved into the depths of themes, narratives, personal storytelling and writing. No matter your destination—professional story, essay, exhibition content or award pursuit—I hope you found the book a worthy companion.

Let hard work and good intentions win both in the work you do and in your writing about it. Above all else, tell your stories well.

ACKNOWLEDGMENTS

A career-long network of colleagues, educators, friends and family members contributed to the knowledge covered in this book. I would be just another blithering, prattling designer author if it were not for the stern yet always humorous knuckle-raps received from my colleague and friend, Michael LeFevre, kind author of this volume's Foreword and contributor of important content to this work.

Gratitude also goes to artist Leslie L. Chekin, who first encouraged me to pull out the writing part of Architect + Action = Result and create a volume devoted to writing, and to Diana Greene, an early writing teacher (now closest of friends) who has provided mountains of support in my many creative pursuits, all beginning with a drawing of my childhood bedroom.

My copyeditor is my fantastic partner-in-crime and husband, George Edmunds, whose support in my career shift from technical research and development for the textile industry into designer over two decades of moons ago facilitated all that has come since. I might also thank the Richmond, Virginia, public school system of his childhood, which ingrained in him an intense awareness of such lost-to-me technicalities as the dangling participle and the past perfect subjunctive.

Thanks go out to the many writing teachers, thesis advisors and fellow authors I've had the honor of working with across over twenty years: Russell Banks, Pinkney Benedict, Lauren Groff, Abby Lipscomb, Fred Lebron, Dan Mueller, Naeem Murr, David Payne, George Saunders, Jenny Offil, Ashley Warlick, and others I'm sure I've lost track of.

Writing, like design and architecture, is best when achieved as a team sport. The myth of the writer in isolation is just that. Any well-written book has many eyes, hands and minds behind its success.

BIO

Rebecca W. E. Edmunds, AIA

Rebecca W. E. Edmunds's career spans multiple disciplines including design for highly technical textiles and apparel. Her design practice focuses on providing leadership in creating consistent, comprehensive communications and writing on design aesthetics and technology. Her experience includes product design for technical applications in environments such as operating rooms, cleanrooms, military and extreme outdoor. She has been a volunteer consultant to state AIA Fellows committees since 2007, aiding their nominees in expressing their cases for elevation to the AIA College of Fellows. Her book, *Architect+ Action=Result,* encapsulates over fifteen years of advice on the Fellowship process.

As president of r4 llc, Edmunds assists professionals, designers and artists in developing comprehensive narratives of their projects, achievements, careers and creative philosophy. She brings a background in design, R&D, graphics, communications and creative writing to professional narrative development. She has served as editor and/or advisor to several publications including *Shaping*

Place (DudalPaine Architects, 2021); *Managing Design: Conversations, Project Controls and Best Practices for Commercial Design and Construction Projects* (Michael A. LeFevre F, 2019); *The AIA College of Fellows History and Directory* (Editor & Researcher, 2019 Edition); *Individual to Collective* (DudalPaine Architects, 2014); *Sketchbook on the World, Pen and Ink Travel Sketches* (Terrance J. Brown, F, 2017 as Prepublication Editor); and *Homelands* (The 2001 NAAB Conference publication, Executive Editor). She has authored and ghost-authored numerous articles and case studies.

Edmunds received a Bachelor of Science from Cornell University, a Master of Architecture from the University of North Carolina Charlotte, and a Master of Fine Arts from Queens University Charlotte. She has completed multiple executive training programs including a mini-MBA at UNC Chapel Hill's Kenan Flagler Business School; Leadership for Performance at UVA's Darden School of Business; and Leadership for Technical Managers at the Center for Creative Leadership.

Edmunds received the 2019 Leslie N. Boney Spirit of Fellowship Award for her work on behalf of the AIA College of Fellows. She has won writing and design awards including the American Institute of Architect's Henry Adams Medal, the AIA NC Designer Book Award, and UNC Charlotte's Excellence in Designer History and Theory Book Award, and Best Designer Design Project. She won an Innovation Award for Technology from now gone textile manufacturer Burlington Industries.

Ingram Content Group UK Ltd.
Milton Keynes UK
UKHW010809190623
423681UK00016B/757